Praise for *Outsider*

"This book is small in size, but huge in spirit. Read it, revel in it, then make your way outside and get some dirt on your clothes."

> — Gregory McNamee, author of *Gila: The Life and Death of an American River*

"What could be better than a pairing of Lawrence Millman and Henry David Thoreau? *Outsider* is a piece to cherish and a reminder that we are never alone as long as words live on the printed page."

> — David Breithaupt, contributor *LA Review of Books*

"If you read Larry Millman (and the gods help you if you don't!), then you already know he is an odd fellow. This sweet and sharp beauty of a bagatelle lets us in on how he got that way, with a good many grins and groans along the way. And it leaves us feeling lucky that Larry, like Henry, has followed his own nose, and no one else's. Long may he veer!"

> — Robert Michael Pyle, author of *Children of the Night* and *The Thunder Tree*

"In a culture gone insane, misfits are our best or perhaps only hope. Two meet in Millman's kaleidoscopic mini-memoir of boyhood days. The mind on display—like Thoreau's—thrills to the tune of nature, drawn by the generally neglected or even despised: slugs, mushrooms, millipedes, earthworms.... Clear-eyed, wild as youth itself, with its hands in the dirt and teeming with life, *Outsider* earns a place on the shelf next to that transcendentalist's essay 'Walking.'"

— Michael Engelhard, author of *Arctic Traverse*

"Outsider is as refreshing as sitting by Walden Pond on a drizzly silver afternoon."

— Eric Paul Shaffer, author of *Green Leaves: Selected & New Poems*

"Millman has unique way of observing nature to better understand the world."

— Richard B. Primack, author of *Walden Warming: Climate Change Comes to Thoreau's Woods*

"Lawrence Millman is that rarest of creatures — a nature writer with a sense of humor. He would have kept his buddy Henry David Thoreau in stitches."

— Jim Christy, author of *The Rough Road to the North* and *Traveling Light*

"Lawrence Millman's idle reflections on a childhood spent with Henry David Thoreau are at once irreverent, enlightening, and entertaining. Thoreau must be clawing at the lid of his coffin to join in on the fun."

— David O. Born, author of *Hypothermia*

"Lawrence Millman is my kind of guy—kind of like a cross between Henry David Thoreau and a badger (the Eurasian badger, as the American badger is sometimes considered ill-tempered). Like Larry, I am always happiest among the salamanders and caterpillars, but reading Larry's vivid, honest, often hilarious accounts of how nature shaped his quirky, abundant life makes for excellent company. Everyone who loves animals and nature will love this."

— Sy Montgomery, author of *Of Time and Turtles: Mending the World, Shell by Shattered Shell*

Also by Lawrence Millman

OUTSIDER

OUTSIDER

My Boyhood with Thoreau

Lawrence Millman

COYOTE ARTS

Library of Congress Control Number: 2024902073

ISBN   Paper   978-1-58775-046-5
       E-Book   978-1-58775-051-9

3 5 7 9 10 8 6 4 2

Coyote Arts LLC
PO Box 6690
Albuquerque, New Mexico 87197-6690
www.coyote-arts.com

"The world has become inaccessible because we drive there."
— Ivan Illich

"Soap and education are not so sudden as a massacre, but they are more deadly in the long run."
— Mark Twain

"If it's obsolete, it works."
— H. W. Tilman

"To be silent the whole day long, see no newspaper, hear no radio … be thoroughly lazy and completely indifferent to the fate of the world is the finest medicine a man can give himself."
— Henry Miller

"The universe is made of stories, not atoms."
— Muriel Rukeyser

"All technology should be assumed guilty until proven innocent."
— David Brower

"One hundred intelligent people in a room only makes one big idiot."
— Carl Jung

Prelude

I'VE WRITTEN THIS BRIEF memoir as a burst of anecdotes rather than a continuous narrative. For that's the way my memory operates with respect to the past: rough-and-tumble rather than smoothly flowing. As for the title, it refers not only to the outdoors being my habitat of choice, but also to the fact that I was (and still am) outside any known social group ... unless you regard mushrooms, insects, or earthworms as social groups. As the subtitle suggests, I spent part of my youth with the naturalist Henry David Thoreau. And not just my youth—in the gloom of the contemporary world, Thoreau stands like a beacon of light to me.

1.

EVEN WHEN I WAS just an army of embryonic cells multiplying inside her, my mother rejected me. To one of her friends, she sent a letter in which she asked, "What did I do to deserve this?" *This* was, of course, me.

Having been provided with what might called a social distancing gene, I always tried to remain apart from most members of my species. A lady friend of mine once asked my mother what I was like as a little boy. "He hated crowds," my mother said, adding, "For him, a crowd was more than one person."

One person would often be one too many. In grade school, a boy who wanted to be my playmate kept leaving all sorts of toy soldiers on my desk. I got so tired of these attempts to buy my friendship that I put a bag of dog shit on his desk, telling him that if he didn't stop bothering me, next time it would be a bag of elephant (or hippopotamus, I don't remember) shit.

I didn't have special needs except for the need to escape from other people … sometimes even from my mother and father. One way of getting away from my parents was gulping down my meals as quickly as possible, but when I did, I would sometimes choke. "Your food went down the wrong way," my mother would explain to me. If I'd been a bit older, I might have replied, "Of course it did, because I'm the wrong way myself."

Brutality is a fetish of boyhood. Boys like to beat up each other, and if one of them did this often enough, he would be declared (what an honor!) the class bully. But if you want to beat someone up, you have to get close to them, and I was distant from the boys who might have wanted to beat me up …

… with one exception. One day after school, a brawny kid with a large wart on his neck followed me as I was walking home, shouting "How come you don't sing Jingle Bells like everyone else?" and "You've got the smallest pee-pee in the world!" After a block or two, I could tolerate him no more, so when I saw a recently run-over squirrel, I picked it up and flung it at him. The dead squirrel struck him squarely in the face, and he ran off crying.

Unlike most kids, I didn't go through a dinosaur phase. That's because I needed to see or touch an animal rather than play with a plastic version of it or encounter its image in a picture book or on a television screen. Nor did I go through a Disney phase. Mickey Mouse? Even a dead mouse interested me more.

Although I distanced myself from Mickey Mouse and his fellow cartoon characters as well as most of my schoolmates, I got up close and personal with snails, snakes, earthworms, slugs, spiders, frogs, millipedes, caterpillars, and salamanders. If something creeped, crawled, or slithered, I regarded it as good company. Likewise airborne creatures such as hornets, butterflies, and even mosquitoes interested me, but airborne human contraptions such as planes or a Sputnik bored me almost but not quite to tears.

Let me add caddis fly larvae to the list of good

company. I would walk down to a nearby stream, pick up one of these larvae, and gaze admiringly at it. Its helical case, a protective covering of pebbles, sand grains, and miniature twigs bound together by silk, seemed to me much superior to any item of human clothing.

My mentor-to-be Henry David Thoreau wrote: "It appears to be a law that you can't have a deep sympathy with both man and nature. Those qualities that bring you near to one estrange you from the other."

Estranged from man (woman, too), I seem to have obeyed that law.

An abnormal level of the hormone oxytocin reputedly makes children less empathetic. But less empathetic toward what? I had a high degree of empathy toward earthworms, which were considered ecological warriors rather than ecological marauders at the time. I would hang out with them in my family's backyard, and with my youthful taxonomic skills, give them names based on my favorite drinks. The lightest ones were vanilla milkshakes, darker ones were chocolate milkshakes, and the darkest ones were chocolate malts.

Our next door neighbor gave me brownies every time I showed up at her door. When I learned that she was moving somewhere else, I gave her a jar of earthworms as a going away present. Knowing how much I liked earthworms, she burst into tears when she saw what was in the jar.

———

As a kid, I spent a quite a bit of my time with earthworms and other ground dwelling creatures in my family's backyard. Often I ended up looking as if my home, like theirs, was dirt. On one such occasion, when I was covered with more dirt than usual, my father said, "You're the dirtiest little boy in the world." These words made my youthful chest swell with pride.

2.

A S SOON AS I learned the trick of writing, I began writing stories. Here is what I recall from two of these stories: a mother tells her son to stay away from rats because they're really nasty creatures, then some rats say to the boy, "Stay away from your mother because she's a really nasty creature;" and an ape regards a fellow named Tarzan as being akin to an invasive species, so it kicks him out of a tree, "*my* tree," it informs Tarzan.

Thoreau said he sustained himself by reading, and from an early age, I sustained myself by reading. too. Running my eyes over the titles of books in my parents' library, I found a copy of Kenneth Grahame's *The Wind in the Willows*. I liked this book so much that I decided to write a thank you letter to its author. "He's dead, so you can't write a letter to him," my father told me. A pity, I thought, because that meant Mr. Toad, Ratty, and Mole were dead, too.

Another book I liked was a collection of fables by the perhaps mythical Greek writer Aesop. I especially liked the fable about the grasshopper and the ants. I identified with the fiddle-playing grasshopper, but not the workaholic ants, since I considered (and still consider) work a four-letter word. I think Thoreau himself would have identified with the grasshopper, for he believed in (as he put it) "one day's work and six days off."

I identified with the grasshopper so much that I wanted it to take up residence under my bed, so I put leaves and insects under my bed for it to munch upon. Every day I would look under my bed, but I didn't see or hear a fiddle-playing grasshopper there. Not even once.

I might not have found a fiddle-playing grasshopper under my bed, but I did see a scruffy fiddle-playing tramp in front of a local grocery store. He seemed to me such a worthy individual that I gave him all the coins in my pocket. He thanked me by playing an off-key tune on his fiddle.

On a trip to the country, I found a four-foot rat snake, and with my parents' consent, brought it home. Soon I was walking around the house with the snake draped around my neck and shoulders. Its tongue seemed to find my body odors just as pleasant as I found its musky smell. One afternoon I walked into the backyard with the snake around my neck, and it quickly dropped to the ground and slithered into a hedge row, disappearing from my life forever.

Since I couldn't have a grasshopper or a snake as a companion, I collected some crayfish from a nearby pond and turned a seldom used bathtub into a home for them. Years later, when our house was sold, the bathtub had to be destroyed, for it had an ineradicable brown ring around its perimeter—a sign that its inhabitants, like me, hadn't given a damn about cleanliness.

If Kipling's Mowgli could engage in bear-talk and bird-talk, I felt I could engage in crayfish-talk, so I would tell my crayfish that they needn't worry, I wasn't going to betray their trust in me by eating them. Or I would tell them how much I disliked my

5th grade teacher Miss O'Rear, who would exile her students to the cloakroom at the slightest provocation.

On one occasion, Miss O'Rear was writing math problems on the blackboard when I saw a spider skittering across the floor. I got down on all fours and followed it. She peered at me through her horn-rimmed glasses and asked me what I was doing.

"Studying a wolf spider," I said.

"This class isn't about spiders!" she shouted at me with a voice like a howitzer, then pointed to the cloakroom …

… where I sat down in the semi-darkness and wrote the following poem: "Miss O'Rear / A kick in the rear / May you disappear / In a bottle of beer / Happy New Year." Not exactly Pulitzer Prize material, but at least it expressed my feelings about this mastodon in petticoats.

Rather than exile me, my mother would often ignore me. An example: we were having dinner in a restaurant, and I said I needed to go to the bathroom.

"Before we left home, I asked you if you needed to go to the bathroom, and you said no, you didn't," my mother told me, then went on eating her dinner.

I couldn't find the restaurant's bathroom, so I went outside and peed against a tree.

Years later, my mother said she still felt guilty about ignoring my lavatorial needs at the restaurant. "It was really awful of me to do that," she told me.

I did my best to console her. After all, she had taught me to answer nature's call in nature itself, an act I now perform whenever possible.

3.

I FOUND A COPY OF Thoreau's *Walden* in the family library, and Thoreau's account of living for two years in a small cabin near Walden Pond soon became the equivalent of a Bible for me. Indeed, I liked the book so much that one summer I pitched a tent in my family's single acre, fenced-in backyard, and became a 12-year-old Thoreau imitator for a week.

I should say that I imitated Thoreau in some ways, but not in others. For example, we had very different diets. He ate peas, potatoes, turnips, beans, and still more beans (he was a passionate cultivator of them), while I ate peanut butter-and-jelly sandwiches, Green Giant corn niblets, Kellogg's Frosted Flakes, graham crackers, and potato chips, washing those food items down with bottles of 7-Up or Dr. Pepper.

———

During my week-long retreat, I didn't take a shower or even wash myself, so instead of calling me "a dirty little boy," my father now called me "a dirty little Thoreau." These words made me feel like I was friends with Thoreau, maybe even a member of his family, so from now on I'll refer to him as "Henry."

———

A short distance from my tent was an old white ash tree. I felt a sense of companionship with this ancient tree, so I refused to climb it lest I somehow wreak havoc on its serenity. But I did answer nature's call against its trunk, and it didn't seem to mind this at all.

———

Also close to my tent was a large white mushroom, probably an *Agaricus* species. Another close companion.

As I later learned, I *did* happen to be close to the mushroom. For phylogenetic analyses of DNA have determined that mushrooms (i.e., fungi) occupy a branch on the tree of life surprisingly close to our own branch.

Henry himself seemed to have been aware of this

when he wrote: "The humblest fungus displays a life akin to our own."

A speculation: fungi, spiders, and snakes trigger a blinding terror or at least a phobic response in rather a number of people, so might this have made me appreciate them all the more? For they were outsiders just as I was an outsider.

In the family garden, I watched lady-bird beetles decorated with red and orange freckles scurry daintily up and down the branch of a rose bush. What pretty girls, I told myself, for I had no idea that some of these lady-birds might have been males.

Upon being released in the backyard, our cocker spaniel would run after every bird, rabbit, or squirrel in sight. Most of these creatures took off at the sight and sound of a barking dog, but one afternoon I watched a squirrel rise up on its hind legs and make a series of angry hissing sounds. Those hisses seemed to say, "Get the hell away from me, you stupid canine." Our dog ran away, whining.

I happened to be on the side of the squirrel, since I had very little affection for such overly domesticated creatures as our family dog. Henry probably wouldn't have been fond of such a brought-to-heel animal himself, for he wrote, "Life consists of wildness," adding: "The most alive is the wildest." He might not have thought Peppy (our spaniel's name) was alive at all.

I often saw robins digging earthworms out of their homes in the ground. Several years earlier, when earthworms were among my closest friends, this sight would have disturbed me so much that I might have tried to scare away the robins, but now I realized that earthworms were as essential to their diet as peanut butter sandwiches were to mine.

One morning I saw a young stiff goldenrod *(Solidago rigida)* with bristly hairs all over its leaves. I thought hairs grew only on mature plants, as they did on certain parts of us humans, so I perused my copy of *Walden,* but found nothing about a stiff goldenrod's hairs in its pages. I guess no one, not even Henry, is perfect, I said to myself. Later I learned that the hairs collected dew in the morning and dripped it down to the plant's roots.

The nearest approximation of Walden Pond in my family's backyard was a stone bird bath filled with water and mounted on a pedestal. During his retreat, Henry wrote, "I am no more lonely than a loon in a pond." During my own retreat, I felt no more lonely than a catbird or a blue jay splashing around in this bird bath.

4.

ONE MORNING DURING MY backyard retreat, I began writing a *Walden* of my own. I used a pencil mostly because Henry made pencils. Only a few sentences from my *Walden* remain in my memory:

"A tall ash tree rises above my short life."

"My tent is a wonderful place—it has no motors, switches, or buttons."

"As the mushroom near my tent didn't eat me, I decided not to eat it."

———

I also wrote a story during my retreat. Entitled "Quivox and the Ghosts," its hero was a Native American named Quivox who finds himself being pursued by a posse of ghosts. Slowly but surely, they're gaining on him. Finally, he turns around and laughs at his pursuers, telling them that they're only ghosts. They're so humiliated by this revelation that they disappear.

I gave my hero the unusual name of Quivox instead of calling him Squatting Bull, Angry Wolf, Kicking Bear, or Raging Buffalo because I wanted to celebrate the letters "Q" and "X." After all, they were outsiders compared to the commonly used letters in the alphabet. I wanted to include another outsider, the letter "Z," in my hero's name, but I couldn't find a place to put it.

My story might have been an attempt to indicate how I felt about television and movie cowboys. These bronc-riding good guys in stovepipe Stetsons who spend their time killing Native Americans and out- laws struck me as stupid macho types. Of course, I identified with the bad guys rather than the so-called good guys.

Concerning television: whenever I watched it, I felt like I was looking at a piece of furniture in- side which tiny loud-mouthed human beings were trapped.

And now I remember another sentence from my

otherwise forgotten personal *Walden:* "How lucky I am not to have a television in my tent!"

At night I would sometimes light a candle inside my tent and play chess with myself. Not surprisingly, I won every game, even those games where I'd make a stupid blunder. I would doubtless have been a much better chess player except—just as in life itself—I seemed eager to make blunders.

"I never found a companion so companionable as solitude," Henry wrote. Even so, he entertained quite a few visitors in his ten-by-fifteen-foot cabin. In my tent, I entertained only a single visitor, a blond-haired girl with large blue-bottle eyes and silky skin who'd been in my English class the previous year. To me, she seemed almost as colorful as a kingfisher or a scarlet tanager

During her visit, the girl planted her lips firmly on mine and gave me the first genuine kiss I ever had. That kiss tasted like a hot dog or a chili-dog, I can't remember exactly which. Shortly after she kissed me, the girl farted. "My ass made that noise!" she exclaimed with an astonished look on her face.

And shortly after she made this exclamation, she said, "I've gotta go home now and watch *I Love Lucy.*"

Truth to tell, I would have preferred another fart.

Henry believed rain has "a fertilizing influence," adding that "the part of you that is the wettest is the fullest of life." I decided to test this idea, so one evening when there was a heavy downpour, I sat outside my tent and basked in the rain while reading a book of stories by Jack London. I got so wet that I became an approximation of Walden Pond myself. What a nice feeling, I thought, agreeing with Henry.

First my mother, then my father came out and asked me if I was okay. Even though I told them I was fine, they wanted me to come indoors right away, as if they thought the rain would either pummel me to death or turn into a raging river and carry me away. When I repeated that I was perfectly happy, they displayed their parental affection by dragging me into the house so I could become (as Henry put it) "a sojourner in civilized life again."

Thus ended my quasi-*Walden* retreat, but only that retreat. When Henry left Walden Pond, he brought Walden with him, and when I went indoors with my parents, I brought the outdoors with me. Since then, I've brought the outdoors with me wherever I happen to go.

5.

MY MOTHER AND FATHER were perpetually at each other's throats, shouting, slamming doors, and locking their proverbial horns. They never used the squishy language of love with each other, nor did they use that language with me. After my mother would go into one of her tirades against me, my father would say, "Don't forget, your mother really loves you." If this is love, I told myself, I don't want to have anything to do with it.

My parents did have one thing in common— they liked to go fishing. They thought I might like to go fishing too, but whenever they took me with them, my line would get entangled with theirs because I was paying attention to the insects, plants, mushrooms, and amphibians in the vicinity rather than my line. After several entangled trips, they didn't take me fishing with them again.

My mother and father had another thing in common—they wanted me to become a social boy. They knew I wouldn't become a member of a fraternity, a book club, or the school's chess club, so they put their temporarily peaceful heads together, and since I liked the out-of-doors …

… they sent me to a summer camp. My cabin was crowded with other boys, so I often slept outside in the woods, and while the other boys engaged in rifle practice, I engaged in archery. Sometimes I shot arrows into pictures of John Wayne, the Lone Ranger, and Roy Rogers that I'd torn from magazines.

During dinner one evening, I overheard one of the camp's counselors tell another counselor that I was a nutcase.

In another effort to make me not only a social boy and maybe even cultivate my masculinity, my father had me fill out an application, and I became a Boy Scout.

On one of our troop's first outings, another Scout lit a firecracker and put it in a bullfrog's mouth, killing the poor amphibian. I was outraged. I told the fellow to be prepared (the Scout motto), because I would stick a lit firecracker in his mouth if he did this again.

The killer relayed my threat to his father, who happened to be the Scoutmaster. The two of us met, and the Scoutmaster chastised me. When I told him that it was worse, far worse to put a firecracker in a bullfrog's mouth than in his son's mouth, he kicked me out of the Scouts.

I could light a firecracker, no problem, but I couldn't fathom mechanical objects such as power switches, motors, burglar alarms, fire alarms, stoves, elevators, toasters, garage door openers, or washing machines. Nor did I make any attempt to fathom them, because they didn't interest me. They probably wouldn't have interested Henry, either. For he wrote. "Let your life be a counter-friction to stop the machine."

I did manage to stop at least one machine. One day I was using a vacuum cleaner to remove the debris from my bedroom floor when it suddenly stopped functioning. My father tried and failed to make it work for perhaps an hour. "It's a mystery," he said to no one in particular. He bought a new vacuum cleaner, and I felt a sense of triumph when he refused to let me use it.

———

Even as I write these words, I'm still hopeless with anything mechanical.

A few days ago the fire alarm went off in my abode, although there was no fire. I couldn't find a way to turn it off, and at last an 85-year-old neighbor lady, hearing the alarm shriek "Fire! Fire! Fire" constantly, came over and turned it off for me.

———

I knew no more about the mechanics of human sexuality than I knew about mechanical objects. One of my schoolmates told me the following joke:

Question: Why can't Santa Claus have children?

Answer: Because he comes down the chimney.

I didn't get the joke, so I told it to my father, and rather than explain its intricacies to me, he ushered me down to the basement and opened a locked file.

———

What was in the file? A bunch of such seemingly indecent books as D. H. Lawrence's *Lady Chatter-*

ley's Lover, Gargantua and Pantagruel by Rabelais, *My
Life and Loves* by Frank Harris, Henry Miller's *Tropic
of Cancer, The Satyricon* by Petronius, *Fanny Hill* by
John Cleland, and Alfred Kinsey's *Sexual Behavior in
the Human Male.*

Thus I learned about the so-called birds and the
bees from reading books instead of in person. I also
learned that a chimney would not have been an ap-
propriate place for Santa's miniature tadpoles, otherwise known as sperm.

6.

A LARGE NUMBER OF MUSHROOMS were fruiting on my high school's football field. Some of them were very delicate, and others looked like the robust one I'd encountered during my Walden retreat. Suddenly I saw the tall, straight-arrow football coach vigorously kicking all of them over—did he think they would interfere with his team's prowess? This murderous deed deprived me of any interest I might have had in football or any other sport …

———

… despite the fact that my father called me "Sport" ever since I could remember. "You should take a shower, Sport," he'd tell me. Or: "Please don't call your mother a witch, Sport." Or: "Chew with your mouth shut, Sport."

———

The football coach was also my gym teacher. At one point he asked me why I didn't want to play football or basketball like other boys.

"Because those sports are against my religion," I told him.

"What's your religion?" the teacher asked.

"Mushrooms," I said, and this disclosure seemed to baffle him.

Later the coach checked my records and then told me that they didn't seem to indicate that my religion was mushrooms. I informed him that I'd changed religions just the other day, which was the reason why the new one wasn't in the records. His baffled look did not leave his face even though he decided to let the matter rest.

Years later, I still have more faith in mushrooms than I have in any deity.

"I'd rather sit on a pumpkin and have it all to myself than be crowded on a velvet cushion," Henry wrote. I was a pumpkin sitter myself, and I tended to poke fun at anyone who wasn't. For example, the Beatles had recently become popular, so I asked a classmate if she was interested in seeing them. She nodded excitedly, so I showed her a jar with a bunch of beetles inside it. She shot me a ferocious look and tried to knock the jar out of my hand.

———

Another pumpkin sitter was a pig-tailed girl who blew her nose on her sleeve and then showed the snot to any guy who seemed to be interested in her, saying, "Cute, isn't it?" Not surprisingly, not a single one of the guys regarded her snot as cute.

———

In my classes, the fear of a Soviet nuclear attack inspired air raid drills during which students were obliged to hide under their desks, lest they be snuffed out by a nuclear bomb. This inspired me to write a story about the Soviets dropping not a nuclear bomb on the U.S., but millions upon millions of Snickers bars, and as folks were busy scooping them up, the Soviets invaded our country and easily conquered it.

———

The Vietnam War was hitting its stride, and I wrote GET THE HELL OUT OF VIETNAM in large India Ink letters across my forehead. This did not go over well with the teachers, most of whom seemed to be in favor of the war. When my American history teacher saw these words, his eyes became pellets of rat poison, and he told me to wash off those words or I'd be expelled. "But I'm against the Vietnam War!" I said. The teacher snarled something in response, then took me to the men's room and washed off the words himself.

I didn't dislike all my teachers, just most of them. One of the teachers I liked was my biology teacher, who once told our class: "Leeches are probably smarter than us, since they have thirty-two brains, and we humans have at most one." It's a wonder that she didn't get expelled for saying this!

My English teacher was giving a lecture on nature-themed books, but he didn't mention *Walden.* I raised my hand and asked him if he had read it. When he said he knew about the book, but hadn't actually read it, I exclaimed, "You must be the only teacher in the world who hasn't read *Walden!*"

Not nice. Not nice at all. I possessed the social skills of an Abominable (to be politically correct) Snowperson, so I couldn't resist paying instant heed to that fractious beast in my thorax known as a heart.

7.

Most boys my age were lifting up the hoods and inspecting the motors of cars, the better to prepare themselves for the glorious day in the not too distant future when they would become the drivers of those cars and thus be able to shout to the world, "Here I come, hell-bent for leather!"

As for myself, a pair of feet were perfectly adequate for my needs—why would I want to replace them with tires? And why would I ever want to undergo such a ridiculous act as drive a gas guzzler along a monotonous cement highway?

"Two or three hours of walking will carry me to as strange a country as I ever expect to see," Henry wrote.

In only a few minutes of walking, I would reach a strange country of my own—the vacant lot almost directly across the street from my home. There I would hang out with rabbits, squirrels, crows, bluejays, spiders, mushrooms, mullein, Russian sage, chickweed, and garter snakes, most of which I would not have seen if I'd been imprisoned in a car.

Since the vacant lot was nature, I found it an excellent habitat for answering nature's call, whereas the inside of a car would not, definitely not, have been a good habitat to answer that call.

My parents wanted me to get a driver's license. So I took the written test and flunked it on purpose.

My mother thought that any kid who refuses to drive a car must have some sort of mental problem. Specifically, she wondered whether I might be autistic, which I assumed meant that I disliked cars (i.e., autos), so she took me to see a therapist.

After our session, the shrink informed my mother that I probably didn't have any sort of mental problem, although I did seem to be something of a misfit. He also told her that I might become an ichthyologist when I grew up. Why did he say an ichthyologist? Because I found the fish in his aquarium much more interesting than his attempt to evaluate my health, and I spent most of the session looking at them.

After my visit to the shrink, my mother showed her devotion to me by shouting these words: "If you don't get a driver's license, I'll make you wash the dishes after our meals.." And my father showed his devotion by saying he'd withhold my allowance unless I got a driver's license. Thus I had no choice but to take the driver's test again, and this time I passed it … on purpose. I could now seal myself off from the world in a two-ton wheelchair!

Later I wrote a story that indicated my feelings about motorized vehicles. A group of Native Americans are leading a traditional lifestyle in some back-country area. One day, in search of game, they venture away, far away from their home and end up on a highway, where they see a large truck blowing white smoke from its exhaust and heading toward them. Assuming it's some kind of god, they walk in front of the truck and bow down to it, and it runs them over.

8.

I N MY SENIOR YEAR in high school, I took a shop class whose power tools were beyond my comprehension. Every time I tried to use one of them, something would go wrong. I once damaged a table saw by accidentally placing the running blade against a metal lathe. Even hand tools seemed to be beyond me. During one of the classes, I stabbed myself with a screwdriver, an act that inspired laughter from my classmates.

Since I tended to wreak havoc both on the class's tools and on myself, the shop teacher didn't mind if I sat on a bench and read books. I read mostly island-related books such as: *Treasure Island* by Robert Louis Stevenson, *Robinson Crusoe* by Daniel Defoe, *The Island of Doctor Moreau* by H. G. Wells, and *The*

Lord of the Flies by William Golding.

Not only do islands play a role in the evolution of certain species, but they also play a role in my own evolution. Since I seemed to be separated from the mainland of humanity, I thought of myself as an island. Yes, I know: the poet John Donne wrote that no man is an island, but he never met me.

I might have been an island, but I also took pleasure in being on real islands. One summer my family took a trip to an island off the Florida coast, and upon first setting foot on that island's seemingly endless beach, I felt like a caterpillar eagerly awaiting its transformation into a butterfly …

…and when I began walking along that beach, I underwent this transformation. My life as a bored high schooler vanished. My parents' desire to control me vanished. Time itself vanished. Even the silhouette of palm trees rising above the beach vanished. All that remained was a bounty of seashells—spiny murexes, magpie top shells, trumpet tritons, emperor helmets, banded tulips, alphabet cones, scotch bonnets, flamingo tongues, angelwings, shark's eyes, calico scallops, and lightning whelks.

The glare of the sun and the glittering waves dazzled my eyes, but did not dazzle them nearly as much as the bounty of shells scattered along the sandy beach. Dare I say that I didn't do any sunbathing?

Given my newfound interest, my parents suggested that I study conchology or marine biology when I went to college, but I had no desire to do so. For my interest in shells resided in the real world, not the walled-off academic one.

Henry would have agreed with me. "What does education do? It makes a straight ditch out of a meandering stream," he wrote.

I often wandered several miles down the beach. On one such occasion, I heard my mother yelling in the distance, "Where the hell are you? Are you lost?"

"I'm not lost! I'm right here!" I yelled back to her.

A few minutes later, she ran up to me and performed a seemingly contradictory act that was one of her specialties—she simultaneously hugged and berated me.

By this time, I had forgiven my mother for not providing me with any nurture, for I realized that if she had given me nurture, I might not have become so devoted to nature.

During my wanderings, I especially wanted to find a rare species called a Juno's volute (Scaphella junonia), a cream-colored shell with a dozen or so spiral rows of brownish dots. My desire to find it was probably because I thought of myself as an uncommon species … or, if not an uncommon species, at least one that marched to the cadence of idiosyncratic drummer.

While my parents were playing a card game one evening, I wrote a story about a man who finds a Juno's volute on a beach. Ah, he says to himself, I can make big bucks by selling this. All at once the sea-god Nepture rises out of the water and grabs the shell from him, saying something like "Don't abuse this shell by selling it." When the man tries to grab the shell back, Neptune dunks him repeatedly in the sea, until the fellow promises never to try and make filthy lucre by selling a shell or anything else that comes from the natural world.

Day after day, I wandered along the beach, and although I found all sorts of other shells, I never succeeded in finding a Juno's volute. This didn't bother me, though. For I had been meandering back and forth not only to my heart's content, but also to my legs' content.

Finale

F LASH FORWARD A NUMBER of years. I was in Concord, Massachusetts, so I decided to pay a visit to Henry's grave in the town's Sleepy Hollow Cemetery and thank Henry for coming to the aid of my outsider self.

How does one thank a deceased person? you might wonder. In the case of Henry, the answer is simple. Although he died of tuberculosis in the year 1862, I felt he was more alive than most of my contemporaries.

As I was (to use one of Henry's favorite words) sauntering around the cemetery, I thought of life rather than death. A crow gave off a loud *c-c-craw!* at my approach. There were quite a few robins hopping around and singing *cheerily, cheer up, cheerily, cheer up,* and a Viceroy butterfly was resting contentedly on top of a gravestone. There were also lavender irises, coltsfoots, sages, sweet ferns, bristle thistles, and a variety of mushrooms.

At one point, I noticed a garter snake slithering among the gravestones. When I followed it, the snake peered up at me, and its flickering tongue seemed to say, What kind of peculiar upright reptile are you?

At another point, I saw a praying mantis with a distended belly that indicated she would soon experience a happy event.

Many of the gravestones hosted green shield lichens, elegant sunburst lichens, and fringed rosette lichens. How much better to have one's final resting place marked by the biodiversity of the natural world than by just a sterile upright stone with (as is often the custom) artificial flowers placed at its base!

With so many distractions, I didn't begin walking toward Henry's grave until it had become too dark for me to climb the knoll on top of which his grave rested. But I wasn't concerned about this. "Pines and birches ... will constitute my second growth," Henry wrote, and since I'd seen a number of these trees during my sauntering, I felt like I'd been hanging out with him.

————————

"Thanks, Henry," I remarked to a tall white pine as I walked out of the cemetery.

❧

Acknowledgements

In addition to Henry David Thoreau, I would like to thank the following individuals for offering me their tutelage both personally and otherwise: John Muir, Rachel Carson, Elliott Merrick, Ann Zwinger, Henry Miller, Pentti Linkola, Wendell Berry, Peter Freuchen, Carol Towson, Jack London, Edward Abbey, Dirk Hillenius, Gerald Durrell, Eugenia Modell, and Elio Schaechter.

About the Author

WRITER, ETHNOGRAPHER, MYCOLOGIST LAWRENCE MILLMAN has made over forty trips and expeditions to the Arctic and Subarctic. His twenty books include such titles as *Last Places, Northern Latitudes, A Kayak Full of Ghosts, Our Like Will Not Be There Again, Hiking to Siberia, Lost in the Arctic, At the End of the World, The Book of Origins, Fungipedia, The Last Speaker of Bear, Foraging with Jeeves,* and the Coyote Arts title *Goodbye, Ice.* He has written for *Smithsonian, National Geographic, Outside, Atlantic Monthly,* and *The Sunday Times* (London). He lives in Cambridge, Massachusetts.

Colophon

THIS BOOK WAS set in Adobe Garamond Pro, one of several serif fonts named to honor Claude Garamond, a sixteenth-century Parisian engraver.

Garamond—originally styled "Garamont"—fonts were based on those cut for Venetian printer Aldus Manutius by his punchcutter Francesco Griffo in 1495. These fonts were designed to mimic the organic style of hand calligraphy, but with a more upright, less slanted look. Early twentieth-century research found that many of the sixteenth-century fonts attributed to Claude Garamond were not his work, but the work of a coterie of punchcutters.

In 2000, a Garamond font was released by Adobe Inc. in a remastered form utilizing the modern Open-Type font format. This font, "Adobe Garamond Pro," is the one used to set *Outsider.*

Coyote Arts

COYOTE ARTS is a literary arts publisher dedicated to the power of words and images to transform human lives and the environment we inhabit. We blend a local focus with a global perspective. We publish works of poetry, fiction, non-fiction, and drama that engage the sense of wonder and possibility. Many of the books have an environmental focus.

We carry on where our previous enterprises—Asylum Arts and Leaping Dog Press—left off, adding a southwest flair and the mischievous nature of Coyote. Our chosen home of Albuquerque is a crossroads, blessed with millennia of pre-Columbian culture and a history entwined with that of Mexico. Despite a fraught 400 years of settler culture, we have at present an opportunity to blend world culture in a place where many cultures have come together.

Coyote Arts Titles

Forthcoming Coyote Arts Titles

And don't miss Goodbye, Ice

In a time of change and uncertainty, Lawrence Millman's *Goodbye, Ice: Arctic Poems* offers a window into the natural world of the Arctic and the tradition-bound indigenous people who have lived there for millennia. Climate change, inevitably, raises its ugly head in many of the poems, but the book is a lament not just for the loss of ice, but for the loss of the Arctic itself.

"Lawrence Millman is a true original who takes no prisoners. His poetry does not ask permission of the kind of people who think they know what 'poetry' is, and as a result it is truer to life — real life — than most of what marches under that banner. These poems come from, and speak for, the reality of Earth as it is."

— Paul Kingsnorth, author of *Confessions of a Recovering Environmentalist and Other Essays*

"From polar bears to pointless missionaries, plagues of cruise ships to mosquitoes, eiders to owls to ravens and the people to whom all of these matter, *Goodbye, Ice* shows as many strands and colors of the polar zones as any Aurora Borealis. You'll rue the warming, yes, but you'll not close the book without laughing too. I love these poems very much."

— Robert Michael Pyle, author of *Wintergreen, Chinook & Chanterelle* and *The Nature Matrix*

"I imagine future archaeologists finding wind-chiseled stones in an Inuit graveyard. On each stone is carved a poem from Lawrence Millman's *Goodbye, Ice,* a book that's equally an epitaph and a celebration for the arctic spirit-world and landscape. Said archaeologists would say, 'So this is what happened here…' — and be haunted by it for the rest of their lives."

— Howard Norman, author of *The Ghost Clause*

"Lawrence Millman's poems take us into the Arctic wilds, introduce us to its icons, its relics, and its cultural curiosities. They bring you mementos from the rapidly disappearing cultures of ice. When he prays, 'May the gods of the tundra grant me lichen until I become lichen myself,' take care. You may become lichen, too."

— Art Goodtimes, author of *Looking South to Lone Cone*

Praise for the Work of Lawrence Millman

"Millman's a genius."

> — Annie Dillard, author of *Pilgrim at Tinker Creek*

"A wonderful writer!"

> — Paul Theroux, author of *The Great Railway Bazaar*

"The master of the remote."

> — Bruce Chatwin, author of *In Patagonia* and
> *The Songlines*

"Lawrence Millman is one of our great storytellers."

> — Tim Cahill, author of *Jaguars Ripped My Flesh*

"Everything Lawrence Millman writes is original, and most of
it is funny and profound."

> — Paul Kingsnorth, author of *Confessions of a Recovering
> Environmentalist*

62219801R00057